P9-BZC-614

IF I REALLY WANTED TO
HAVE A GREAT MARRIAGE,
I WOULD . . .

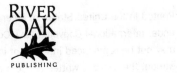

Unless otherwise indicated, all Scriptures are taken from
the *Holy Bible, New International Version* ®. NIV ®.
Copyright © 1973, 1978, 1984 by International Bible
Society. Used by permission of Zondervan Publishing
House. All rights reserved.

Scripture marked TLB is taken from *The Living Bible.*
Copyright © 1971. Used by permission of Tyndale House
Publishers, Inc., Wheaton, Illinois 60189. All rights reserved.

Scripture quotation marked KJV is taken from the *King
James Version* of the Bible.

*If I Really Wanted to Have a Great Marriage,
I Would . . .*
ISBN 1-58919-775-5
Copyright © 2001 by RiverOak Publishing
P. O. Box 700143
Tulsa, Oklahoma 74170-0143

Manuscript prepared by Susan Downs, Canton, Ohio

Printed in the United States of America. All rights reserved
under International Copyright Law. Contents and/or cover
may not be reproduced in whole or in part in any form
without the express written consent of the Publisher.

Introduction

A great marriage requires a good deal more than a ceremony ending with a kiss and a certified license. A great marriage demands nonstop nurturing, mutual attention, constant cooperation, joint effort, abundant affection, two-way communication, and a heaping helping of hard work.

Wherever you turn, you see marriages dissolving into divorce; couples once head over heels in love now snarl and snipe at one another. What steps can you take to protect your marriage against such a fate? Whether you are newly married or celebrating your golden anniversary, the gentle reminders found in this little book can assist you in strengthening your commitment to your mate and creating a *great* marriage—a marriage made to last "'til death do us part."

May God bless you both with a future filled with marital bliss.

Have a Great Marriage,

I Would . . .

Hold out
my hand.

*I am always with you; you
hold me by my right hand.*
—Psalm 73:23

Following the death of a spouse, many a bereaved widow laments the fact that no one touches her anymore. Seldom—if ever—do people complain that their spouse touched them too much through the years.

Begin now to build a large reservoir of "touching" memories to cherish in your golden years. Extend your hand across the dinner table and give your mate's hand a gentle squeeze. Intertwine your fingers as you walk down the street. The simple act of touching costs nothing and requires little effort yet pays big dividends if practiced faithfully. Your tender touch can convey love and a multitude of other positive emotions.

Reach out and touch the one you love.

Have a Great Marriage,

I Would . . .

Take a vacation from television.

The easiest way to find more time to do all the things you want to do is to turn off the television.
—O.A. Battista

Many people can't imagine living without television. Turning off the tube for good constitutes a drastic lifestyle change that few can manage cold turkey. Better results come when they wean themselves in smaller doses, starting with one day or even one evening. It also helps to plan a pleasant activity to enjoy together. Try reading a book together or engaging in a lively conversation on a topic of mutual interest.

Once you've broken the habit of automatically turning on the set, you will be able to practice the lost art of conversation. Spending time discussing the big things and the little things that are happening in your lives will bring a renewed intimacy to your relationship. The number of topics you find to talk about may surprise you. You just may discover that your lives are every bit as interesting as those of your favorite sitcom characters.

Television is a poor substitute for life.

Have a Great Marriage,

I Would . . .

Treasure our "alone" time.

*There is no more lovely,
friendly, and charming
relationship, communion, or
company than a good marriage.*
—Martin Luther

We often go to great lengths to protect our valuables. We polish our silver and wax the car, rent a safe-deposit box for the diamond brooch we inherited, and insure our possessions for the full replacement value. Yet we often neglect one of our most priceless treasures. A strong marriage demands an investment of time spent together—polishing and protecting, nurturing and affirming.

Don't underestimate the value of a good marriage. It can provide you with a lifetime of comfort and encouragement and a strong sense of family even after the kids are grown and gone. But marriage requires constant maintenance, regular one-on-one "alone" time. Don't allow the urgencies of a busy day to crowd out the care of your relationship. Don't allow anything or anyone to interfere with those precious few moments you find to spend alone together.

A great marriage is worth protecting.

Have a Great Marriage,

I Would . . .

Suggest we take a walk together.

*Do two walk together unless
they have agreed to do so?*
—Amos 3:3

Go ahead! A stroll through the neighbor-hood will do both of you good in more ways than one. If you have children at home, saddle up the stroller or strap on their in-line skates. Walk just fast enough to get your heart pumping but not so fast that you can't talk comfortably. Share the details of your busy day. Chat with neighbors. Watch as the sun sets. Saunter in silence and soak in the fresh air and the comforting sense of belonging to each other.

Convenient excuses *not* to walk abound— the weather is too hot, too cold, too rainy, too dry. But you will quickly find that this new evening ritual is worth the effort. It provides an opportunity to exercise your body and your relationship. Don't put it off.

*Spend at least a few minutes
of each day outdoors together.*

Have a Great Marriage,

I Would . . .

Read a book
with my mate.

*The pleasure of all reading
is doubled when one lives
with another who shares
the same books.*
—Katherine Mansfield

Put aside the daily paper filled with depressing news. Instead, go to the nearest library or bookstore on an exploratory mission with your spouse. Search until you find a book that both of you would enjoy. Reclaim the long-forgotten pleasure of reading for enjoyment's sake. You'll find almost endless possibilities as you wander through the shelves—how-to manuals, mysteries, biographies, or classics. Perhaps your mate would enjoy listening to your favorite childhood tale.

The fresh insight, information, and inspiration the two of you can glean from just a few minutes of daily reading will expand your base of shared experiences and provide new topics of conversation as well.

Enrich your mind. Read a book.

Have a Great Marriage,

I Would . . .

Talk, listen, talk, listen, talk, listen . . .

*When you talk you are only
repeating what you already
know—but if you listen
you may learn something.*
—J.P. McEvoy

What a boost to your self-esteem to know that the one person in this world you value most is truly interested in your thoughts, opinions, and feelings. The give-and-take of communication is the nourishment that causes a marriage to grow and thrive.

Never assume that you know what your spouse is thinking or feeling. Care enough to devote your undivided attention. Hear what is being said. Don't simply nod as you mentally formulate your next response. Few compliments surpass the tribute of your genuine interest. For even better results, try putting your spouse first. Reverse the order of this bit of advice to: Listen, talk, listen, talk, listen, talk.

Pay your spouse a tremendous compliment—pay attention!

Have a Great Marriage,

I Would . . .

Pray with
my spouse.

*"Where two or three come
together in my name,
there am I with them."*
—Matthew 18:20

Never do two souls intertwine so closely as when they bow together in prayer. Inhibitions are set aside and a hallowed and holy tenderness transpires between a husband and wife who mutually recognize their need for, and dependence upon, God's intervention and blessing in their lives and marriage.

Today, take your spouse's hands in yours and offer a prayer to God. Begin by saying, "Thank You." You have so many reasons to be thankful! Jointly present your burdens, cares, and concerns to God. Ask for His wisdom to meet the challenges of the day. Solicit His help. Invite the Almighty into your lives.

Cement your marriage with the bond of prayer.

Find a hobby
we can share.

*People who cannot find
time for recreation are
obliged sooner or later to
find time for illness.*
—John Wanamaker

How long has it been since you found a fresh, new interest to share with your spouse? Rather than devoting precious leisure time to separate hobbies, look for activities that you and your mate both enjoy. Pursuing mutual hobbies and interests will turn your attention away from the stressful, hectic routines of everyday life and give you a chance to relax together.

Motorcycling. Golfing. Bird watching. Hiking. Stamp collecting. Fishing. Skydiving. Dominoes or tiddledywinks. There is a hobby tailor-made to fit every couple's budget, schedule, and energy level. You may simply need to experiment with several before you find the perfect hobby for the two of you.

Have the time of your life
with the love of your life.

Refuse to speak negatively about my spouse to others.

*A word rashly spoken
cannot be brought back by
a chariot and four horses.*
—Chinese Proverb

A public forum is not the appropriate place to nurse a grudge. Even if your spouse deserves your criticism, never air your anger and resentment in the company of others. Such an action often backfires.

As the afternoon TV talk shows have proven, an audience is more likely to inflame rather than quell an already volatile situation. When you criticize your mate publicly, you not only lower the listener's estimation of your mate, you lower their opinion of you as well. Stop before you speak those negative words. Ask yourself, *What is it I hope to gain by being critical of my spouse to others?* You'll find that question rarely has a worthy answer.

Disagreements should be discussed behind closed doors.

Never go to bed angry.

*"In your anger do not sin":
Do not let the sun go down
while you are still angry, and
do not give the devil a foothold.*
—Ephesians 4:26-27

Like mushrooms growing in a dark and damp forest, anger sprouts into full-blown contempt during the night. Something about those long, dark hours seems to breed malice. Each tick of the clock intensifies a nighttime rage. Anger is a natural human emotion, but left to fester, it can do real damage to a relationship.

Don't take your anger to bed with you, clutching it close. Don't allow bitterness to fester until it does lasting harm. Expose your anger to the light as soon as it sprouts. Talk openly with your mate about the issue in question. Then forgive and do it quickly. Otherwise, it will be even more difficult in the morning.

Put anger to rest before you retire for the night.

Say, "I'm sorry."

An apology is the Super Glue of life. It can repair just about anything.
—Synn Johnston

Contrary to the memorable line from the movie *Love Story,* sometimes love *does* mean having to say you're sorry. A sincere apology is not a sign of weakness. On the contrary, the act of acknowledging that you are at fault will strengthen your marriage and your spouse's admiration for you.

Don't let pride and stubbornness stand in the way of sincerely apologizing when you are wrong. We all have need of absolution at times. When those times come, the strength of your marriage will rest on your willingness to make things right with those six little words: "Please forgive me. I was wrong."

Nothing can replace a quick
and sincere apology.

Have a Great Marriage,

I Would . . .

Block out time on my calendar for a date with my mate.

The unfortunate thing about this world is that good habits are so much easier to give up than bad ones.
—Williams Somerset Maugham

Before you mark any other dates on your weekly planner, reserve a standing date night with your mate. Schedule this appointment as you would any important business meeting. Free nights seldom, if ever, magically appear. If your calendar or bank account won't allow for a weekly date, aim for a monthly rendezvous.

If you find it next to impossible to pencil in a Friday-night-at-the-movies date, consider a Saturday morning breakfast date at your favorite restaurant or a Sunday afternoon stroll through the park. Once you've mutually decided on the most convenient date, time, and place, religiously guard this important tryst. Don't let anything or anyone squeeze into this time.

Continue a romantic courtship
long after your wedding day.

Have a Great Marriage,

I Would . . .

Eat dinner
at the table.

*When you have eaten and
are satisfied, praise the LORD
your God for the good
land he has given you.*
—Deuteronomy 8:10

Are you always eating on the run? Tonight, will dinner amount to grabbing a quick burger from a drive-thru? If so, you're missing out on an opportunity to communicate with your mate.

As often as possible, share your meal at the table in the quiet of your own home. Don't plan a big production, or your sit-down dinner plans will seldom come to pass. The good china lends a nice touch but isn't necessary. Let the answering machine pick up your calls. Listen to soothing music rather than the blaring TV. Light candles to add a bit of romance to the room. Provide a relaxing atmosphere for your evening meal and watch it become nourishment for your marriage as well as your body.

If you're too busy to sit down and eat—you're too busy.

Have a Great Marriage,

I Would . . .

Agree to

disagree.

*We all live under the same
sky, but we don't all have
the same horizon.*
—Konrad Adenauer

Few issues are worth a long-running feud or a heated debate with your mate. It's best to simply accept that you will not see things from your spouse's point of view at times. Perhaps your differences of opinion center around a political viewpoint or a philosophical stance. Even the most perfectly matched couple should not expect to see eye-to-eye on everything.

When a disagreement surfaces, ask yourself: *Is this matter one in which we will ever be able to agree? Could this disagreement have a significant impact on our marriage? Is it worth the conflict that our relationship would have to endure?* Some battles are worth fighting. Others are not. Pick your battles carefully.

Don't sacrifice your marital bliss for trivialities.

Head off
to bed with
my spouse.

Bed is a bundle of paradoxes:
We go to it with reluctance,
yet we quit it with regret.
—Charles Caleb Colton

Can you recall those sweet days of childhood when your parents lovingly tucked the covers under your chin and kissed you good night? Even though you're all grown up now, those treasured, end-of-the-day feelings need not end. Institute a nightly ritual of "tucking in" your mate.

Don't leave your spouse dozing on the sofa as you tiptoe off to bed. Choose to go off to bed together. Save at least enough energy to kiss your mate and whisper "good night" on those evenings when you are both too tired for a romantic interlude. Dozing off together will increase your feelings of well-being and give you a head start on a good night's sleep.

A bedtime ritual need not end with childhood.

Avoid the appearance of evil.

*Abstain from all
appearance of evil.*
—1 Thessalonians 5:22 KJV

A lunch date with a coworker of the opposite sex may be strictly business. The late-night work session that includes the two of you may be legitimate. Nevertheless, if your actions cause others to raise a suspicious eyebrow, beware. Steer clear of any circumstance that might create even a twinge of jealousy in your mate.

We live in a time when these precautions may be ridiculed by some as straight-laced nonsense. But keeping your actions above reproach is a guardian against temptation and misunderstanding. It allows your spouse to rest more securely in the constancy of your love and faithfulness. No business matter is more important than your marriage.

Trust never fails when integrity prevails.

Have a Great Marriage,

I Would . . .

Ask God to protect and direct my spouse.

*Heaven is full of answers
to prayers which no one
ever bothered to ask.*
—Billy Graham

How often do you think about your spouse in the course of a day? Each time your thoughts turn to your mate, institute a new habit—pause long enough to breathe a prayer on his or her behalf.

Do you know of specific problems or issues your spouse is facing? Petition God for a special impartation of wisdom and guidance. Pray for special protection from any harm. Ask God to bless your mate with joy and peace in spite of life's difficulties. Before you say "Amen," thank God for allowing you to share your life with such a special person. Open your heart to supernatural insight into how you might increase your love.

Prayer brings you close even when you're apart.

Have a Great Marriage,

I Would . . .

Tell my spouse what I need.

*Understanding human
needs is half the job
of meeting them.*
—Adlai Stevenson

As the years go by, it's easy to grow lazy in regard to our verbal communication, thinking that our mate automatically knows how we feel. It is an unfortunate characteristic of many long-term relationships. But couples engaged in great marriages have learned to overcome it.

Regardless of how good at mind reading your spouse may seem at times, only you can really know what's going on inside your head! Leave nothing to speculation or assumption, no matter how in tune with your thoughts your mate may seem to be. Put your thoughts into words. Assuming that another person—no matter how close—understands all of your needs, wants, and desires is foolhardy at best. Talk things over. Communicate.

Lack of communication
leads to unmet expectations.

Have a Great Marriage,

I Would . . .

Choose my spouse as my best friend.

*For this reason a man will
leave his father and mother
and be united to his wife, and
they will become one flesh.*
—Genesis 2:24

An advice column in a popular women's magazine recently published an unusual inquiry. A bride-to-be wanted to ask her best friend, a man, to be her "maid" of honor in her upcoming wedding. She wanted to know the proper term for a man serving in this capacity. A better question for this woman might have been, *What hope does my marriage have for survival if the man I marry is not my best friend?*

Your marriage should encapsulate the ultimate of every earthly relationship. Your mate should be your best friend, your most trusted confidant, the first—and final— person you turn to when you need advice, comfort, and love. Is your spouse your best friend? If not, start working on that today.

Friendship is the foundation
of every great marriage.

Have a Great Marriage,

I Would . . .

Keep a positive outlook on life.

*When I complain, I do it
because "it's good to get
things off my chest"; when you
complain, I remind you that
"griping doesn't help anything."*
—Sydney Harris

A single complaint often leads your thoughts down a depressing spiral of negativity. Negativity breeds faster than rabbits. Rarely does a complaining attitude produce positive results.

No matter how well things are going, most of us can find something to complain about. It is so easy to fall into the habit of negative thinking. Determine today to put an end to sour negativity and instead look for ways to improve your attitude. Commit a random act of kindness. Focus your attention away from your problems and onto the needs of others. Bless your spouse and those around you with a cheerful disposition.

A positive attitude engenders
a positive response.

Have a Great Marriage,

I Would . . .

Attend church with my spouse.

Let us not give up meeting together, as some are in the habit of doing, but let us encourage one another— and all the more as you see the Day approaching.
—Hebrews 10:25

By joining with like-minded believers in corporate worship, not only will your soul gain nourishment, your marriage will be strengthened as well. Here are just a few of the benefits church attendance offers a couple after they say "I do."

Church:
- Provides spiritual instruction and guidance.
- Turns your thoughts to the truths of Scripture.
- Brings to light areas of your life that may be contrary to Christian teaching.
- Develops your spirit's sensitivities and ability to love.
- Provides outlets for ministry and involvement in other people's lives.
- Focuses your attention on the majesty of God through worship and prayer.
- Empowers you and your mate through the development of personal faith in God.

Share a spiritual meal—go to church.

Have a Great Marriage,

I Would . . .

Brag about my spouse to family and friends.

*I can live for two months
on a good compliment.*
—Mark Twain

Your parents may feel that your mate doesn't quite live up to the high expectations they held for you. Your friends may view the one you married as an intruder. But when you consistently highlight the positive attributes of the love of your life, your praise should eventually wear down even the most stubborn skeptic.

Seize every opportunity to point out the many wonderful qualities you see in your mate. When you go overboard with genuine praise, the rewards are twofold: You reinforce for yourself how fortunate you are to be married to such a fantastic person, and you let others know you are not willing to entertain any criticism of your spouse.

Focus not on the warts but on the wonders of your mate.

Put my spouse above my work.

*There is a time for everything,
and a season for every
activity under heaven.*
—Ecclesiastes 3:1

Do you constantly work late? Do you put in long hours of overtime and drag through your home each night exhausted? When you go out for dinner with your spouse, are your thoughts on the office rather than on the conversation? In subtle and not-so-subtle ways, your job may usurp your mate's rightful place in your priorities. The balancing act between vocation and family often proves tough to manage.

Your career may serve as more than just a means of earning an income. If so, that's wonderful for you! But when your job takes precedence over your family, it's time to reexamine your priorities. Both husbands and wives should view marriage as their first career.

Marriage is the most important job you'll ever hold.

Have a Great Marriage,

I Would . . .

Stroll through the mall arm in arm with my spouse.

*Imparadis'd in one
another's arms.*
—John Milton

These days, when divorce and discord prevail in many American homes, perhaps the time has come for happily married couples to exhibit a little PDA (Public Display of Affection). Rarely do we see spouses express genuine love and wholesome affection these days. Our world needs a few sweet reminders that true love within marriage can—and still does—last a lifetime.

Take pride in the fact that you are beating the odds. Use appropriate expressions of tenderness toward your mate wherever you go. But don't be surprised if you hear a few "ahhhs" as you pass by.

Let the world see your love.

Have a Great Marriage,

I Would . . .

Express my innermost fears to my spouse.

*The only thing we have
to fear is fear itself.*
—Franklin D. Roosevelt

Whatever anxiety you harbor—whether wildly irrational or distinctly possible—your best first step is to bring it out into the light. Trust your spouse enough to share your darkest secret worry. Through the simple act of admitting your inmost anxiety, you begin to break the stranglehold it has on you.

Let your spouse comfort you and tell you everything will be all right. Join hands and hearts in prayer about your fear and trust God to help you in your time of need. It's quite possible that this action will allow your spouse to share his or her own fears. This action will bring you closer together and provide a wellspring of comfort and affirmation as you attempt to overcome your fears and walk in faith.

To overcome fear, you must expose it.

Have a Great Marriage,

I Would . . .

Avoid verbal sparring, especially in public.

*Better a dry crust with peace
and quiet than a house full
of feasting, with strife.*
—Proverbs 17:1

Even if you and your spouse fuss in apparent lighthearted fun, save the feuding for behind closed doors. When you constantly pick at one another in public, those observing you may begin to wonder how you treat each other when no one else is around.

Another public faux pas is contradicting your spouse. By correcting your mate in front of others, your audience begins to doubt your spouse's credibility. And your contradictory comments might be viewed as disloyal. As your spouse recounts a shared experience to others, bite your tongue if you are tempted to say, "Hey, I don't remember it that way." Wait until the two of you are alone.

Save disagreements and contradictions until you get home.

Play an active role in monitoring my spouse's health.

*All wealth is founded on health.
To squander money is foolish;
to squander health is murder
in the second degree.*
—B.C. Forbes

Teaching your mate new health habits can be difficult. For some reason, many people resist that type of interaction with their mate. However, it's too important to simply ignore. Consider buying a family health-club membership as a Christmas gift this year. Gently remind your spouse when it's time for a checkup and be willing to go along for moral support, if necessary.

If your mate could stand to shed a few pounds, suggest that you diet together. At the very least, don't eat ice cream and cake when your spouse is around. By resisting the urge to nag or bully, you can do a lot to encourage your spouse to eat better, get plenty of sleep, and exercise.

Postpone "'til death do us part"
as long as you can.

Have a Great Marriage,

I Would . . .

Take care of my own health.

*Health is not valued
until sickness comes.*
—Thomas Fuller

If no one bothered to check and change the oil in the family car, the engine wouldn't last very long. Proper care and attention are also required for your body to function properly. Neglect may go unnoticed for a while, but eventually poor maintenance will catch up with you.

Few of us take care of our bodies with the same diligence we give to our automobiles. We are either running on empty—skipping meals while racing through a stressful day—or we are filling up with bad fuel—those empty, sugar-filled calories. Stop long enough to schedule some routine maintenance. Fill your body with "high-octane" foods. Slow down to a reasonable speed. It's difficult to invest in your marriage if you are sick or constantly exhausted.

Honor your body by giving it the care it needs.

Have a Great Marriage,

I Would . . .

Find ways to minimize interruptions during our together times.

*"They are no longer two,
but one. Therefore what
God has joined together,
let man not separate."*
—Matthew 19:6

The hours you and your spouse spend together one-on-one are precious. Whenever possible, you should plan to tune out interruptions. That can be particularly challenging during the child-rearing years but not impossible with a little advanced planning.

Children are not the only interruptions, of course. For a little while each day, turn off the TV, let your machine answer the phone, and decide not to answer the door. Couples who want to have a great marriage must be willing to make the time to focus completely on each other. Regular alone time builds a firm foundation for a lasting relationship.

Stand firm in your resolve for "alone" time.

Have a Great Marriage,

I Would . . .

Plan a romantic getaway.

*You will never find time
for anything. If you want
time you must make it.*
—Charles Burton

A woman gave her husband a note he was to read as he left the office one day. He was to open the glove box of his car and read these instructions: "Pull out of your office parking lot and go three miles south. Turn left. Go 4.3 miles. Turn right . . ." and so on. Her husband was delighted when he arrived at the mystery destination. The directions led him to a hotel where his wife had planned a romantic getaway.

If you wait for a convenient time to break away with your mate, that time may never come. Why not arrange your schedule to include a mini-retreat this month?

Romance is the flame that keeps marriage exciting.

Have a Great Marriage,

I Would . . .

Compliment my spouse often.

To say a compliment well is a high art, and few possess it.
—Mark Twain

Don't hold back. Let your mate hear complimentary words from your lips every day. Rather than criticism, use your words to praise and build confidence. Point out the physical attributes you find attractive. And continually remind your spouse of the many reasons you are sure you married the right person.

Toss aside any fears you might have about building up your spouse too much. The world outside your door can be a belittling and demoralizing place. Make your home a refuge from society's steady rips. Let your spouse know that your eyes see the wonderful things that the world never notices. Your eyes are filled with love.

Declare yourself as your spouse's No.1 fan.

Have a Great Marriage,

I Would . . .

Not expect my spouse to meet all my needs.

My God will meet all your needs according to his glorious riches in Christ Jesus.
—Philippians 4:19

A good marriage demands reliance upon one another and a mutual effort to satisfy life's demands. However, even the most devoted couples aren't capable of meeting each other's needs completely.

Surround yourself with a safety net of relationships—close friends and extended family—in order to stay emotionally healthy. Making your spouse exclusively responsible for meeting every emotional, physical, and spiritual need can kill even the most promising relationship. Acquire at least a basic knowledge of how to survive should your spouse be gone for an extended time. And remember to rely upon God alone—not any human being—to satisfy your soul's deepest needs.

No one but God can meet all your needs.

Offer to attend an activity my spouse enjoys.

*If you want peace in the home,
do what your wife wants.*
—African Proverb

If you really want to invest in your marriage, offer to join your spouse on an outing of his or her choice—and go cheerfully. Make no demands. Accept no reciprocal agreement. Whether this means whooping it up at a ball game or spending a few hours at a craft mall, this should be a "no strings attached" exercise done simply for love.

Don't stand in the shadows tapping your foot and impatiently glancing at your watch. Join in and make an effort to understand what your spouse enjoys about the activity. Purchase a special treat to celebrate the day. You may discover as you head for home that you enjoyed the day just as much as your spouse did.

No time is wasted when it's spent making another person happy.

Have a Great Marriage,

I Would . . .

Kiss, hug, and say, "I love you!"

*Let him kiss me with
the kisses of his mouth.*
—Song of Songs 1:2

The world beyond the walls of your home can be a less-than-loving place. In fact it can be downright vicious at times. Both you and your mate may drag in the door after a hard day's work with ragged and worn-down spirits, feeling emotionally bruised and abused. Your words can serve as a healing balm to the wounded spirit of your mate—and this soothing cure is sure to spread to you as well.

Guard the daily ritual of a good-bye kiss as you head your separate ways each morning. Come together each evening with a warm embrace. Say sweet words of love every chance you get.

Don't leave your affection to speculation.

Have a Great Marriage,

I Would . . .

Remember that my marriage is my most important relationship.

Grow old along with me!
The best is yet to be,
The last of life, for which
the first was made.
Our times are in his hand.
—Robert Browning

Parents often succumb to the temptation to pour all of their energies and attentions into their children. Then when the day comes that the kids are gone, Mom and Dad can only stare at each other blankly, with nothing left in common.

Take care that the parent-child relationship does not supersede your relationship with your spouse. Keep alive mutual interests apart from your children. Commit to a thirty-minute conversation at least once a week in which you don't even mention the children. Regularly participate in activities that you will enjoy together long after the kids have gone out on their own.

Make your marriage your first priority.

Encourage giggling.

*A good laugh is
sunshine in a house.*
—William Thackeray

Few people actually laugh themselves to death, but many do succumb to stress-related illnesses like heart attack and stroke. A healthy dose of humor can make a significant contribution to your overall health and well-being, including your marriage relationship.

Science is learning what common sense has shown us all along: Laughter is wonderful medicine and an important aid to healing. It revitalizes and relieves tension. No matter what problems you face today, look for humor and share a healthy chuckle or two with your mate.

*Exercise your laugh muscles
and shed some stress.*

Keep private things private.

*Now it is required that
those who have been given
a trust must prove faithful.*
—1 Corinthians 4:2

Trust is a fragile thing—hesitantly gained, quickly lost. The personal revelations, insecurities, and innermost thoughts that you and your mate share within your marriage represent a sacred trust. The secrets divulged between husband and wife during intimate moments of communication must be guarded at all cost.

You hold within your grasp the ability to crush your spouse's spirit. By sharing a single one of these private disclosures, you weaken your mate's confidence in you. Protect this information with the impenetrability of an armored truck. Ask yourself before you speak, *Would my mate feel comfortable with my sharing this? Is it something I'd say if my spouse were here with me?*

Secrets between husband and wife are sacred.

Have a Great Marriage,

I Would . . .

Take care
of my
appearance.

*Personal appearance is
looking the best you
can for the money.*
—Virginia Cary Hudson

In all likelihood, before you were married you went to great lengths to make yourself presentable to your future mate. You stood in front of the mirror combing and re-combing your hair until it looked just right. You used large quantities of mouthwash and deodorant and liberally applied your favorite cologne. Often these efforts are ignored when our dating days come to an end.

The energies you applied to "catching" your spouse should not be abandoned now. Go to the trouble of making yourself look good. Shave or apply fresh makeup. Keep yourself presentable and do your best to remain as attractive as you were when you first fell in love.

Honor your mate by looking your best.

Understand what my spouse does for a living.

Every man's affairs, however little, are important to himself.
—Samuel Johnson

Chances are, your spouse leads a double life—a life at home and a life at work apart from you. Once you say good-bye to one another in the morning, you head off to separate worlds filled with people and tasks that will still be affecting your moods and attitudes when you come back together in the evening.

For a full and healthy marriage, take time to understand and converse with your spouse about the daily challenges he or she faces on the job. Accompany your spouse to company functions and meet coworkers with enthusiasm. Without becoming a pest, strive to know the world your spouse lives in apart from you, and encourage him or her to enter into your workday world.

Your work life is too important not to share.

Have a Great Marriage,

I Would . . .

Refuse to keep score.

*Bear with each other and forgive
whatever grievances you may
have against one another.
Forgive as the Lord forgave you.*
—Colossians 3:13

Whether you have been married fifty years or five months, you and your spouse have a history. And, undoubtedly, somewhere in that history lurks instances of insensitivity on the part of your mate. Perhaps he or she spoke harsh words in an angry moment or acted less than loving at a time when you needed love the most.

Often, couples haul in the heavy artillery of past grievances when they enter a fresh battlefield. Such tactics only add fuel to the fight and never aid in the peacekeeping effort. So before your next conflict, make an agreement with your mate. Agree never to insert past issues into today's conflicts. Stay in the present tense when you face marital disagreement.

Don't keep a list of "wrongs remembered."

Have a Great Marriage,

I Would . . .

Value my spouse's opinion.

*We are of different opinions
at different hours, but we
always may be said to be at
heart on the side of truth.*
—Ralph Waldo Emerson

In those times when you search for wisdom, where are you likely to turn? A pastor? A psychologist? Both may be excellent options. Don't rule out either of these resources. But before you go searching for a wise sage, seek the opinion of your spouse.

So often we fail to fully appreciate those with whom we are most familiar. Their insight appears commonplace when we're around them constantly. What a shame! These are the very people who have a vested interest in our happiness and success. Don't foolishly disregard this important resource. Place a high value on your spouse's opinion.

The best counsel you ever get may come from your own home.

Have a Great Marriage,

I Would . . .

Keep a journal of our favorite shared memories.

*God gave us our memories
so that we might have
roses in December.*
—Sir James Barrie

Certain moments should be cherished forever. Yet as time passes, our memories fade and fail. Think back. Can you still vividly recall how your spouse acted on that first date? Do you remember the soft, sweet words the two of you shared privately on the night before your wedding?

Years from now, the mere reading of a yellowed-with-age journal entry can transport you back in time to a special event. And when the going gets rough, a reminder of happier times may provide that extra "oomph" you need to succeed. Make your memories last a lifetime. Write them down.

Maintain a written record of your marriage's memorable moments.

Have a Great Marriage,

I Would . . .

Accept my spouse without reservation.

*Accept one another, then,
just as Christ accepted you,
in order to bring praise to God.*
—Romans 15:7

Many people spend their entire lives searching for acceptance. Whether or not they felt accepted by their parents may have a lot to do with their searching and constant attempts to measure up. A marriage is the one place where we should expect to feel unconditionally loved.

Your spouse must not sense that you are always trying to mold him or her into your ideal of the perfect mate. Avoid comparisons. Accept your spouse without stipulations or demands. Grant permission for your spouse to be real, unfettered, and relaxed.

Love with terms and conditions
isn't really love at all.

Have a Great Marriage,

I Would . . .

Keep no secrets.

*The man who can keep
a secret may be wise, but
he is not half as wise as the
man with no secrets to keep.*
—Edgar Watson Howe

Secrets and lies drip at the back of our thoughts like a leaky faucet, making a good night's sleep nearly impossible. In the darkness, they consume our every thought and rob us of all mental energy.

To appease your conscience, you may adhere to the old saying, "What they don't know won't hurt them." And in some cases, this adage may be true. But secrets can certainly hurt *you.* Truthfulness, confession, and disclosure, no matter how painful they may be, hurt much less than the destruction brought about by dishonesty. Harbor no secrets. Don't tell lies—even little ones. Hide nothing from your mate. Live in total honesty.

A strong marriage and a
clean conscience go hand in hand.

Have a Great Marriage,

I Would . . .

Appreciate the little things my spouse does.

It has long been an axiom of mine that the little things are infinitely the most important.
—Sir Arthur Conan Doyle

Too often when two people live together for an extended period of time, they begin to take each other for granted. Little kindnesses have a way of becoming expectations. When these expectations aren't met, resentment can set in.

Practicing an attitude of gratefulness is a good way to keep a fresh appreciation for the little things your spouse does to care for you and your family. It serves as a reminder to say, "Thank you," and keeps your spouse feeling that his or her actions on your behalf are noticed. Gratefulness is a great boost to marital happiness.

A little appreciation goes a long way.

Have a Great Marriage,

I Would . . .

Dream big dreams with my spouse.

*No eye has seen, no ear has
heard, no mind has conceived
what God has prepared
for those who love him.*
—1 Corinthians 2:9

Dreams of future possibilities inoculate us from despair. They remind us that no matter how depressing our present circumstance, there is potential for a brighter tomorrow. Dreams encourage our spirits and keep us looking up.

Shoot for the moon as you consider the direction you want your lives to take. Join with your mate in exploring a universe full of future destinations. Then live today expecting that someday your dreams will come true. The results may surprise you. Shared dreams lead to shared optimism, shared opportunities, and very often, shared fulfillment.

Two can dream bigger and accomplish more than one.

Learn to laugh at myself.

*He who has learned to
laugh at himself shall never
cease to be entertained.*
—John Powell

When you're in a hurry, have you been known to make some silly mistake, such as spraying hair spray where the deodorant should go or vice versa? Look for the humor in your absentmindedness rather than grimacing in embarrassment. Have a healthy laugh at your own expense.

People who can laugh at themselves make better marriage partners. They tend to be more flexible, tolerant, and well adjusted. Laughing at yourself keeps your ego in check and your feet on the ground. If you've never learned to laugh at yourself, find out why—a strong marriage depends on it.

Refuse to run from your own humanity.

Have a Great Marriage,

I Would . . .

Commemorate important dates.

*I've a grand memory
for forgetting.*
—Robert Louis Stevenson

Red-letter days such as Valentine's Day, birthdays, and anniversaries aren't really very likely to slip by unobserved. When they do so regularly, it is more often the result of carelessness and insensitivity than forgetfulness.

Remembering those dates without being reminded will make a big impression on your spouse. Why? Because it indicates that you deeply value the relationship. It reaffirms your love and emphasizes your commitment to keep your marriage fresh and grounded. These special occasions should not be treated as just more dates to remember. They should be honored as opportunities to celebrate your marriage.

Memorialize the milestones of your marriage.

Have a Great Marriage,

I Would . . .

Fight fair.

*A hot-tempered man stirs up
dissension, but a patient
man calms a quarrel.*
—Proverbs 15:18

Disagreements are inevitable in any marriage. Arguments occur between the most loving mates. In a moment when calm and reason prevail, make a pact to always play by the rules. Your mutually agreed-upon list of rules may read something like this:

- Neither party shall resort to or threaten violence in any form.
- Neither party shall run home to mother.
- Neither party shall sleep on the couch.
- Either party may request a brief cooling-off period to regain emotional control, but the time period should be measured in hours, not days or weeks.

Your list should be unique to the two of you, but once you make your list, play fair. Abide by the rules.

Forgiveness is sweeter than revenge.

Have a Great Marriage,

I Would . . .

Make a list of things I love about my spouse.

*How do I love thee?
Let me count the ways.*
—Elizabeth Barrett Browning

You might as well face the facts. You won't necessarily feel attracted to your spouse when you gaze into his or her sleep-matted eyes in the morning. You may need an occasional reminder of what you ever found attractive in the first place.

Prepare now for the day when the mystique of marriage fades and the excitement melts into commonplace. Keep a record of all the reasons you fell in love with your mate. Add to your list regularly and freely share your insights. You are likely to find that your spouse rewards you by working hard to preserve those things you appreciate most.

Use your words to rekindle your love.

Have a Great Marriage,

I Would . . .

Pick up
after myself.

*What separates two people most
profoundly is a different sense
and degree of cleanliness.*
—Friedrich Nietzsche

Are yesterday's clothes draped across the treadmill? Has the mail accumulated on the credenza so long that the pizza coupons have expired?

When frequently needed items aren't put away properly, chances are you're spending countless minutes of your life frantically searching for them when you're ready to walk out the door. Even worse, if your spouse takes the responsibility of picking up after you, he or she may resent the implication that your time is intrinsically more valuable. Clean up your own clutter, and you're likely to find more minutes in your day—and a more cheerful spouse.

Expecting someone else to clean up after you is irresponsible.

Have a Great Marriage,

I Would . . .

Guard my spouse's need for rest.

*"Come to me, all you
who are weary and burdened,
and I will give you rest."*
—Matthew 11:28

A good nap is a treasure these days. If yard work and home maintenance don't interfere with our need for sleep, the kids or the telephone will. We cram so much into each day that we rarely find time to unwind. But adults still need to get proper rest. Without sufficient downtime, no one can function at peak capacity.

If you want to see true appreciation in your spouse's eyes, suggest that the two of you take a nap together. Resist the urge to fill every minute of your weekends with chores and errands. If you can't take a nap together, offer to keep things under control so your spouse can chill out for an hour or two. You'll be surprised as you see how many ways your kindness makes things better for everyone in the family.

The whole world looks
brighter through rested eyes.

Have a Great Marriage,

I Would . . .

Allow my spouse the benefit of the doubt.

*At the gate which suspicion
enters, love goes out.*
—Thomas Fuller

Jumping to conclusions can land a couple smack-dab in the middle of a sticky relational mess. Accusations and questions of loyalty can drive a deep wedge between mates, virtually halting any real communication.

Mistrust without cause often reveals your own insecurities and jealousies. But what are you to do when such feelings stab at your confidence in your mate? When you catch the first whispers of suspicion, discuss them with your mate immediately. Ask his or her advice on ways to deal with your uncomfortable feelings. Reinforce your trust while confessing your own insecurities. Focus on "me" and "I." Refrain from pointing the finger and leveling blame with an accusatory "you."

Your trust in your spouse is only as strong as your trust in yourself.

Realize that people have different ways of showing love.

The heart has its reasons which reason knows nothing of.
—Blaise Pascal

A pie made from scratch may be a wife's deepest expression of love, while a husband may show his love by cleaning the garage. If your way of showing love is vastly different from your mate's, consider the training ground of his or her childhood. How did your spouse's parents express love in the home? Did they openly show affection or did they express their love in more subtle ways?

Our ways of expressing love are as different as our personalities. Our backgrounds influence our ability to convey the emotions of our hearts. Should you start to feel insecure about your spouse's love, consider the possibility that he or she is simply expressing devotion in ways unfamiliar to you.

Marriage is the union of two very different human beings.

Have a Great Marriage,

I Would . . .

Share chores and do more than my share.

Two are better than one, because they have a good return for their work.
—Ecclesiastes 4:9

Life gets dirty. The management of a household, no matter how small, entails a never-ending cycle of chores. Sit down together and draw up a list of jobs for each of you. Some couples divvy up the workload by assigning one spouse all outdoor chores, while the other handles the work inside the four walls of the house. Others like to share chores inside the house and out. Determine what works best for you.

Don't become resentful when your spouse leaves something undone. Do the task cheerfully and don't make a big deal of it. Make a conscious effort to maintain a proper heart and attitude, serving each other lovingly.

Sharing chores is a tangible way to show love.

Have a Great Marriage,

I Would . . .

Cherish the everyday moments.

*Life is what happens
to you while you're busy
making other plans.*
—John Lennon

We bide our time between vacations and holidays, eager for the next special event on the calendar to roll around, when we should be savoring each moment of our time on earth. The lion's share of life isn't composed of holidays and special days. We do most of our living in the ordinary, everyday here and now.

In the course of a long-term marriage, there are many special occasions. But more than anything else there are the ordinary days that make up your life with your spouse. Don't wait for a special occasion to notice your spouse's smile or thank God for bringing you together. Enjoy each moment.

With each breath you take,
give thanks for your mate.

Spend our money wisely.

*Beware of the little expenses.
A small leak will sink
a great ship.*
—Benjamin Franklin

A wealth of financial books abound, but the best advice regarding fiscal responsibility can be summed up in the following words:

- Don't let your outgo surpass your income.
- Save or invest 10 percent of your take-home pay.
- Before resorting to credit purchases, ask yourself if this item will outlive the debt.
- Live simply. Downsize if need be.
- Put God first with your finances. Give a tithe of 10 percent to your local church.
- Don't stretch your budget so thin that you can't assist those in need.
- Cling loosely to material things. Instead, invest your life in that which transcends earthly wealth.

*Keeping money under control
keeps a marriage strong.*

Be nice to my spouse's coworkers.

*If it is possible, as far
as it depends on you, live
at peace with everyone.*
—Romans 12:18

You know that awful grouch your spouse works with—or for? The one who leaves your mate frustrated or irritated by the end of the day? Even if you never meet your spouse's coworkers face-to-face, you can play an important role in his or her workplace relationships.

Don't be quick to judge or criticize. Encourage your spouse to verbalize the positive characteristics of those he or she works with. Suggest ways to build bridges and mend fences. Most of all, resist the urge to reinforce hurt feelings by taking on your spouse's sense of offense. Your lives will be happier and your marriage stronger when you make a habit of encouraging each other to do the right thing.

Be an example to one another
of love and good works.

Have a Great Marriage,

I Would . . .

Give a special gift—just to say, "I love you."

Let him that desires to see others happy, make haste to give while his gift can be enjoyed, and remember that every moment of delay takes away something from the value of his benefaction.
—Samuel Johnson

Be on the lookout wherever you go for fun trinkets and small gifts for your spouse. The presents need not be expensive purchases or time-consuming projects. Think in terms of items that will make your loved one smile. It can be something as simple as a magazine that you picked up while in the checkout line at the grocery store.

Focus your extravagance on the presentation—not the gift. Prepare a short speech that expresses your heartfelt sentiments. Let your spouse know you bought the gift simply as a reminder of your love. Little things can make a big difference in the life of your marriage.

Gifts from the heart are priceless—
no matter the purchase price.

Have a Great Marriage,

I Would . . .

Willingly seek outside help when it's needed.

It can be no dishonor to learn from others when they speak good sense.
—Sophocles

There may come a day in your marriage when you and your mate reach an impasse. You feel like giving up. Your problems appear too big to solve, and you can't agree on anything. But before you throw in the towel, explore every available option for help.

Your marriage is the most precious human relationship you'll ever know. Preserve it no matter the cost. Unless you are in physical danger or your emotions are so volatile that you may cause harm to your spouse, commit to stick together and work things out. Enlist the aid of a pastor or a professional counselor as you work to mend your marriage and make it strong again.

Marriage is a treasure worth
salvaging, regardless of the sacrifice.

Speak softly even when I'm angry.

A gentle answer turns away wrath, but a harsh word stirs up anger.
—Proverbs 15:1

In the heat of battle, a whisper can be more effective than a shout. If your voice chokes with emotion and intensity, your words may lose their meaning. You may cease to be heard. The ability to maintain a calm and steady demeanor when you feel provoked to yell requires a great deal of self-discipline.

Rather than turning up the volume when you're angry, practice the art of a well-placed pause. Maintain your composure. Count slowly to five—ten, if need be. Often your measured words and calm demeanor will calm your spouse as well. Discover the dramatic results of a soft response.

Wise words softly spoken carry a powerful punch.

If I Really
Wanted to

Have a Great Marriage,

I Would . . .

Sing my spouse's praises in front of our kids.

What children hear at home soon flies abroad.
—Thomas Fuller

Children draw comfort from knowing their parents admire and respect one another. They feel secure when they see Mom and Dad grounded in their love. When you point out the good qualities of your spouse and expound on the reasons for your love, you give your children an increased sense of security, while reinforcing the standards you want your children to seek in a husband or wife. The ideals and expectations your children have for their future marriage partners are built upon what they see lived out by their parents each day.

Brag about your mate. Hold your spouse up as a model for your children. Reserve your gripes and complaints for your personal journal and hold your tongue when you're tempted to criticize.

Light the way for future generations—let your love shine.

Have a Great Marriage,

I Would . . .

Cook to

please.

One cannot think well,
love well, sleep well,
if one has not dined well.
—Virginia Woolf

Express your love in edible ways by taking time to prepare your spouse's favorite foods. Cooking up a great meal of special treats is a powerful reminder to your mate that you are thinking loving thoughts. Even if you have no culinary skill, you can brew the morning's first pot of coffee.

Plan time out of your busy schedule to prepare one of your spouse's favorite foods. Don't wait for the next special occasion. Add fresh meaning to the term "comfort food." If you don't happen to be a great cook, get creative. These days there are many ways to put a delicious meal on the table.

Food prepared by loving hands satisfies more than hunger.

Have a Great Marriage,

I Would . . .

Celebrate our differences.

I praise you because I am
fearfully and wonderfully made;
your works are wonderful,
I know that full well.
     —Psalm 139:14

God knew what He was doing when He made the first human prototypes. He made us male and female—different by decision and design. Our strengths and weaknesses dovetail through a divinely inspired plan. This is especially true in a strong marriage relationship.

When you are tempted to scratch your head in dismay and mumble, "Why does my mate act that way?" realize that the two of you were created to complement each other. Your differences add strength and uniqueness to your marriage. Capitalize on the opportunity to prove that the whole really is greater than the sum of its parts.

Marriage is an opportunity to complete each other.

Watch my weight.

*The one way to get
thin is to reestablish
a purpose in life.*
—Cyril Connolly

Our population is ever increasing in weight. Have you joined this growing crowd? Before you admit to dieting defeat and sink your teeth into another piece of chocolate cake, consider the negative impact your surplus weight may have on your marriage.

Excess weight robs your body of both mental and physical energy. Moreover, a poor self-image created by extra pounds can cause a loss of confidence and leave you feeling unattractive to your mate. That can't help but dampen your romantic interest. Excess weight can shorten your life and damage your health, putting your future lives together at risk. If you've tried without success, ask your doctor for help.

Proper exercise and diet are
a sign of honor to your mate.

Have a Great Marriage,

I Would . . .

Hold my spouse's family in high regard.

*Nobody who has not been in
the interior of a family can say
what the difficulties of any
individual of that family may be.*
—Jane Austen

In-law jokes abound. But extended-family conflicts are no laughing matter. They quickly create stress and disharmony in marriage and can make life miserable. Often the problems we face with our in-laws could be avoided simply by showing them a little courtesy and a lot of respect.

In every conversation concerning your spouse's family, keep your comments positive. Leave the skeletons in the closet where they belong. Refrain from making your mate's mother the brunt of your jokes. Don't criticize Dad. Refuse to belittle or poke fun, no matter how unusual your mate's relatives seem to you. Remember that your spouse's family is now your family as well.

Loving someone means loving who they love.

Resist the urge to nag— always.

*A nagging wife annoys
like constant dripping.*
—Proverbs 19:13 TLB

Even though women usually get the blame for nagging, men are often just as guilty. Nagging may be the single greatest contributor to that dreaded ailment, selective hearing. Before you accuse your spouse of never listening to you, ask yourself if you are guilty of being a nag.

If your badgering produces a payoff now, beware. Even the most compliant mate will eventually tune out a demanding whine. Few people want to be known as a henpecked husband or a browbeaten wife. Harping and hounding seldom produce the desired result. Gently present your request. Say it once. Then wait. Allow plenty of time for your spouse to respond before broaching the subject again.

Designate your home as a no-nag zone.

Have a Great Marriage,

I Would . . .

Plan for
time apart.

*The best thinking has been
done in solitude. The worst
has been done in turmoil.*
—Thomas A. Edison

Regardless of the close relationship you share with your mate, there are times when you both need time alone. Human beings need personal space from time to time in order to grow and thrive. Solitude is necessary to secure peace of mind.

Set aside some time each week for processing deep thoughts and letting your mind and imagination soar. Look at it as a private retreat to refresh your parched soul. If all else fails, lock yourself in the bathroom and soak in the tub for a while. Reconnect with your inner self. Urge your spouse to do the same. Those brief, quiet moments will do you both a world of good.

Retreat. Refresh. Refuel.

Say yes
more often.

*Life is either a daring
adventure or nothing.*
—Helen Keller

Complacency is detrimental to life and marriage. But with each passing year comes an ever-increasing tendency to play it safe. We nestle ourselves into a comfortable routine and refuse to budge without putting up a fight.

Refuse to trudge methodically through another day with nothing of note to mark the passing of time. Set those fuddy-duddy ways aside and throw caution to the wind. Choose something daring for the two of you. Then talk it up to your spouse until he or she catches the vision. Behave unpredictably. Above all else, resist the temptation to conform to the mundane. Say yes to life and a more exciting marriage.

Seize the day! Just say yes!

Be there in the hard times.

*Your words have supported
those who stumbled; you have
strengthened faltering knees.*
—Job 4:4

On that joyous day when you said, "I do," the prospect of troubled times seemed far away. You eagerly committed to stay faithful through the "poorer" part of "for richer or poorer." Without a second thought, you signed up for the "sickness" side of "in sickness and in health." You agreed to remain loyal through the "worse" portion of "for better, for worse."

But when those inevitable dark-cloud days descend, will you keep your promises? Are you more than a fair-weather mate? True faithfulness requires your support and encouragement, not just your physical presence. Refuse to attack with "I told you so," even when the taunt applies. Stand firm in your promise to weather every storm.

Storm clouds are the test of true commitment.

Present a united front in parenting.

*Unity makes strength, and,
since we must be strong,
we must also be one.*
—Grand Duke Friedrich von Baden

"Mom would let me eat ice cream if she were here," the child pleaded. "No," came the father's firm reply. The child pulled out the heavy artillery by turning on the tears. At this, Dad delivered the classic response, "Stop that crying right now, or I'll give you something to cry about." The boy issued his final threat through pouting lips, "I'll tell my mommy on you!"

If you are a parent, the moral of this story is obvious to you. Kids constantly work at evening the odds—and they sometimes outsmart us. Establish the ground rules for cooperative parenting long before your kids can talk. Stick together. Parenting issues can breach even the strongest marital relationship.

United parenting results in better kids and better marriages.

Have a Great Marriage,

I Would . . .

Develop our own secret language.

*The best of life is conversation,
and the greatest success is
confidence, or perfect
understanding between
sincere people.*
—Ralph Waldo Emerson

Creating a secret language doesn't mean you have to study linguistics or enroll in a language institute. You and your spouse have undoubtedly already developed quite a vocabulary. Pause a moment and think. When you're in a crowd, do you trade private glances that hold meaning to no one else? Do you have pet words that require your own secret code to decipher?

That unwritten dictionary, shared only by the two of you, provides a private means of communicating that no one else can translate. Silent signs such as a crinkled nose or crooked grin exchanged at just the right time serve to strengthen the bond of your relationship with your mate.

The language of love needs little interpretation.

Have a Great Marriage,

I Would . . .

Show respect for my parents.

*Honor your father and your
mother, as the LORD your
God has commanded you.*
—Deuteronomy 5:16

We may espouse very different views than those of our parents. We may live vastly divergent lifestyles. Regardless of how much or little feel we have in common with the people who raised us, we all retain a certain number of our parent's characteristics. A part of them resides in us. When we respect our parents simply for who they are, we also are showing respect for ourselves.

This attitude toward your parents sidetracks resentment and allows you to set legitimate, realistic boundaries for the relationship. Erratic, emotional reactions to parental expectations can be as stressful for your spouse as they are for you. Take the lead by determining to show respect for yourself and your parents.

You need not agree with your parents in order to respect them.

Have a Great Marriage,

I Would . . .

Never take my spouse for granted.

*Always leave home with
a tender good-bye and loving
words. They may be the last.*
—Anonymous

Every day you live is a gift from God. Your home, spouse, children, job—even your life—are only on lease to you. You cannot know with certainty how long each lease will last. Therefore, if you've been blessed with another day, you have great reason to rejoice.

Anyone who has watched a spouse endure a life-threatening illness would tell you to daily celebrate the life of the one you love. Put aside petty disagreements. Let your spouse know how much you appreciate the blessing of sharing another day together. Life offers no guarantees, so don't take your life or your spouse's life for granted.

Thank God for your spouse every day.

Grant my spouse some privacy.

*The human animal needs a
freedom seldom mentioned,
freedom from intrusion.*
—Phyllis McGinley

Not everything in marriage is community property. Grant one another some privacy. Don't resent or intrude on the need for personal space. If letters arrive addressed to your mate, resist the urge to open them. Impose a no-snooping rule. Don't eavesdrop on private conversations. Treat as sacred the secret contents of personal journals or diaries. That box of childhood memories and treasures should remain untouched until your mate is ready to share it with you.

When your spouse willingly reveals information, you will know that you have earned true trust—one of the most important elements of a strong marriage. Don't try to rush it. Building trust takes time, but it's well worth the effort.

A happy marriage includes respect for personal space.

Have a Great Marriage,

I Would . . .

Learn to
compromise.

Agree with one another so
that there may be no divisions
among you and that you
may be perfectly united
in mind and thought.
—1 Corinthians 1:10

No marriage can survive without some give-and-take from both parties. The literal meaning of the word "compromise" is "together to promise." You promise and give in just a bit. Don't always insist on having your every wish or demand fulfilled. If you give in once in awhile, you will find the promise of a happy relationship.

Your marriage vows are a commitment to reach a point of togetherness. This means giving, submitting, and letting go of your own demands. A great marriage is one that brings together two independent and different individuals and makes them one. United in purpose, their spirits become intertwined so closely that they become one entity.

Compromise allows two people to become one.

If I Really
Wanted to

Have a Great Marriage,

I Would . . .

Develop mutual friends with my spouse.

The ornaments of our house are the friends who frequent it.
—Ralph Waldo Emerson

In the course of a marriage, both partners will make friends. We all need to have and keep personal friendships. However, we also need to develop friendships with other couples. These relationships offer a marriage something that a personal friendship cannot.

Strong relationships with other couples offer you an opportunity to reach out to others together. They enable you to participate in activities with friends without being apart. Best of all, they represent a close group of friends with a vested interest in the success of your marriage. Seek out and nurture these precious friendships.

Making friends together draws you closer.

Have a Great Marriage,

I Would . . .

Remember what's important. Forget what's not.

Now these three remain: faith, hope and love. But the greatest of these is love.
—1 Corinthians 13:13

Many of us become stressed out over things that really won't matter when all is said and done. Step back long enough to evaluate your life priorities. Will the issues that eat at your thoughts today still matter a year—or five years—from now?

When we reach the end of life's journey, few of us will complain that we didn't accumulate more possessions. Neglected relationships and selfish attitudes will prove to be our deepest regrets. Prioritize the things that truly matter in life. Spend time nurturing family and friends. Give your marriage the attention it deserves. Reflect on your relationship with God. All of life's other urgencies take a backseat to these.

Don't let the urgent replace the important things of life.

Additional copies of this book
are available from your local bookstore.

The following titles are also available
in this series:

If I Really Wanted to Grow Closer to God, I Would . . .
If I Really Wanted to Be Happy, I Would . . .
If I Really Wanted to Simplify My Life, I Would . . .
If I Really Wanted to Lose Weight, I Would . . .
If I Really Wanted to Make a Difference, I Would . . .
If I Really Wanted to Be a Great Friend, I Would . . .
If I Really Wanted to Beat Stress, I Would . . .

If you have enjoyed this book,
or if it has impacted your life,
we would like to hear from you.

Please contact us at:

RiverOak Publishing
Department E
P.O. Box 700143
Tulsa, Oklahoma 74170-0143

RIVER
OAK
PUBLISHING